MASKED MAN, BLACK

Masked Man, Black

Pandemic & Protest Poems

by
Frank X Walker

Accents Publishing • Lexington, Kentucky • 2020

Copyright © 2020 by Frank X Walker
All rights reserved

Printed in the United States of America

Accents Publishing
Editor: Katerina Stoykova-Klemer
Cover Image: Frank X Walker, *Fit the Description*, Acrylic on Canvas, 1992

Library of Congress Control Number: 2020947066
ISBN: 978-1-936628-59-9
First Edition

Accents Publishing is an independent press for brilliant voices. For a catalog of current and upcoming titles, please visit us on the Web at

www.accents-publishing.com

CONTENTS

Introduction / vii

Silver Linings / 1
Commencement 2020 / 2
The Walking Dead / 4
If There Was No More Anything … / 5
Bad Medicine / 6
Half the Treasure I Won … / 7
Baptism by Dirt / 8
To the Ten-Year-Old Kid on a Ventilator / 9
Before Hashtags / 10
Old-School Math / 11
On Mother's Day / 12
Severe Weather Warning / 14
B.C. / 15
Peculiar / 16
Hairline Fracture / 17
Mendacity / 18
Mrs. Butterworth, Uncle Ben & Aunt Jemima / 20
Complicit, at Most / 21
To the White Women Who Formed a Line … / 22
The End of Sporting / 23
Read a Book, Then Ask What You Can Do / 24
Offensive Captain / 26
Qualified Immunity / 28
Twelve Things Amy Believed She Knew / 29
Sleight of Hand / 30
Ode to Meat Packers / 31
Easter Prayer, 2020 A.C. / 33
Fake News? / 35
Mamasorri School / 36
I'm Being Sarcastic / 38
Combustibles / 39
Deejay Battle / 40
Y'all Say I Do, We Say Black Lives Matter / 42
The Faithful / 43

A New Word Order / 44
Colonizer-13 / 45
Dirty Dozen / 46
Masked Man, Black / 47
To the Man Who Wore a Klan Hood to the Grocery Store … / 48
To the Man Spewing Spit and Vitriol in the Trooper's Face … / 49
Hypocrites and Oaths / 50
Want Ads / 51
Season Ticket Holders / 52
Too Soon? / 53
Exodus? / 54
Stormy Forecast / 55
A Joyful Noise / 56
The Apprenticeship Wreck / 57
Citius, Altius, Fortius, A.C. / 58
Scientific Doubt / 60
Like Moby-Dick, but Bigger / 62
Six Feet Under, Six Apart / 63
Revisionist History / 65
Remember to Breathe / 66
O Death / 67
Laissez les Bon Temps Rouler / 69
2020 Vision / 70
Corona Love / 71

Acknowledgments / 73

About the Author / 75

INTRODUCTION

> We wear the mask that grins and lies,
> It hides our cheeks and shades our eyes,—
> This debt we pay to human guile;
> With torn and bleeding hearts we smile
>
> —Paul Lawrence Dunbar

> Like men we'll face the murderous, cowardly pack,
> Pressed to the wall, dying, but fighting back!
>
> —Claude McKay

In the tradition of bearing witness, Frank X Walker's *Masked Man, Black* moves us through the many phases of this era marked by a global health crisis and uprisings for racial justice. With echoes of Claude McKay's "If We Must Die," a sonnet written in the time of pandemic and in response to the infamous Red Summer which saw white supremacist violence perpetrated against Black communities across the United States, Walker connects us to a painful past and illustrates its links to our present. Never leaving us in despair, anger, or anguish, however, the poems help us to reflect, hope, and join in a demand for a different world. This collection is a time capsule, but not one that we ever want to bury away in the backyard. Rather, it beckons us to open it again and again as we attempt to understand the current state of our nation and this world. Moreover, its deeply personal and, at times, intimate provocations place us as readers into the familiar worlds of these poems. There we find moments of joy and comfort in the midst of fear and anger. We laugh, too. At times we are left with the residue of some innominate but recognizable thing which leaves us questioning.

In form and content, these poems boast an aesthetic of the people. Like viscera on the page, they reach deep inside and cry out for us when we cannot gather up the words ourselves. They engage the socio-cultural and political climate which continues to shape family, place, and identity, and they excavate an often uncomfortable or disturbing history. Of course, these are themes in which Walker's visual and literary art have long been rooted. Beginning with *Fit the Description*, Walker's original art on the cover, as well as with the title poem of the collection "Masked Man, Black," we are reminded:

> But It Isn't new.
> All the chalk outlines are white.
> All the states are red.
> The coronavirus doesn't discriminate.
> Racists still do.

The poem's use of color and murder imagery illuminates the linkages between the failures of national governance and the racist transgressions of the brutal carceral system. Similarly, the likening of COVID-19 to a destructive meteorological event in "Severe Weather Warning" uses metaphor and metonymy to emphasize the human impact while signifying the lack of consequences for the structural authority.

> COVID-19, a silent multi-eyed system, formed in early 2020,
>   made landfall, and stalled out over NYC, Chicago, Detroit,
>   and New Orleans causing the closing of schools,
>   churches, the cancellation of all sporting
>   and entertainment events, widespread
>   damage to the economy and catastrophic
>   loss of life, though physical structures,
>   shorelines, and trees have sustained
>   zero damage.

Even as these poems employ sophisticated literary devices, they remain anchored in the aesthetic of people and our lived experiences. The poem "Deejay Battle" captures the losses of the moment as it evokes a Black summer concert tradition. Lifting up the new sounds of summer—music in the voices of uprising and revolution in the streets—it shouts an indictment:

> Know justice. Know peace.
> No justice. No peace.
> No just ICE raids.
> No guilty cops, just us,
> dead, dying, and chalk marked

over and over again,
like some wack DJ, rewinding
the bridge or dead refrain,
scratching   at our eyes

with already viral
breathless black body porn
professionally made
by the hands, feet and now knees
of thug police, again

Similarly, poems like "Want Ads," "On Mother's Day," and "Old-School Math" call for a deep and abiding empathy. They illustrate our humanity with nurturing echoes, reminding us that "poor, broken, and old / did not mean indignity. / And it certainly didn't equal death."

Frank X Walker's poems do not hesitate to engage the discomforting realities of our world. *Masked Man, Black* is a bold book of poetry, never blanching in its pursuit of truth and justice, always laying bare our individual and collective strife, consistently reaching for love as a sustaining force—whether it be communal, familial, sensual, spiritual, or otherwise. In these pages, you will encounter lines which unsettle, you will see images that sadden, you will hear sounds that arouse, you will feel pain and pleasure, you will taste this moment along with its past and its future.

Shauna M. Morgan, Ph.D.

For Keith, Breonna, Bill, Chadwick and the countless others stolen away in 2020

SILVER LININGS

Remembering you actually like
your family, love your partner
and being outdoors barefooted.

Finishing the unread stack of books,
cooking without using a microwave,
and writing letters longhand.

Noticing that watching, listening,
or playing in the rain feels
the exact opposite as driving in it.

Meeting the old you, the cloud-watching
wannabe gardener, before time clocks
and hurry, bills and worry made you

a prisoner, took your life hostage,
replaced it with cable,
a big screen, and a remote control.

COMMENCEMENT 2020

> "... ground yourself in values that last, like honesty,
> hard work, responsibility, fairness, generosity,
> [and] respect for others"
>
> —President Barack Obama

I had a grandson in the class of 2020,
the first high school class born after 9/11.
Yo-Yo Ma played "Simple Gifts"
and a little Bach No. 6 on national TV for him
and all his classmates across the country.

Ma, on cello, was followed
by a slate of musicians I had never heard of:
Dua Lipa, Bad Bunny, and H.E.R.

A whole platoon of famous athletes, actors,
musicians, CEOs and former presidents
showed up to congratulate them,
to applaud their advocacy and service, to salute
their passion, resilience, patience, and creativity,
to send them off, to urge them to "demand better,"
to officially hand them the keys to the future.

And why not? Who else has inherited so many
school shootings? Who else has been more invested
in climate change? Who else uses our terrifying work
tools as toys to upload their joy on TikTok?

After three years of the current administration,
its anti-education Secretary, and Zoom physics
and calculus, they need no mandate
to change the world.

They already started with at-home proms,

drive-in theater graduations and middle-of-main
street parade-style processionals. Only parents
are afraid they'll spend the best years of college
the same way they finished senior year.

In truth, adults have broken a lot of shit.
Let's not get in the way while they endeavor to fix it.

This class will be forever special, if for no other reason,
and despite the partisan divide modeled by adults,
the whole damn country graduated   together.

THE WALKING DEAD

Week one.
you heard it was a hoax.

Week two:
they took your venti latte
with extra something or other.

Week three:
you left the room
without a phone
in your hand
—and survived.

IF THERE WAS NO MORE ANYTHING ...

but waiting,
could you stare out the window
at courting wrens and sit
on your porch
and just listen to spring?

Could you find yourself
dragging loved ones
out of bed, just to watch
the sun rise?

BAD MEDICINE

If contracting the coronavirus
was a death sentence initially transmitted
via cheap Walmart blankets
or attached to a lie that originated
in the White House, it might never
have been placed at the feet of the Chinese.

The *I Ching* and *Revelations* would both agree
that it most likely came from the Navajo,
or the Cheyenne, or the Sioux.

The joint chiefs would be trying to explain
to the Commander-in-Cheat
exactly why it would be a bad idea
to drop a nuclear bomb
on Pine Ridge or Standing Rock
or Cherokee, North Carolina.

Montezuma's revenge
would become a mere footnote in history.
And next to karma in the dictionary
it would just say, "see COVID-19."

If marginalized populations
are most at risk during this pandemic
imagine what's happening on the Rez,
because it will not be on your evening news.

HALF THE TREASURE I WON ...

in the custody battle
is dribbling two basketballs
at rapid speed
on the front porch.

Her twin is converting
the front steps
into chalk stained-glass windows
with her younger cousins.

The older ones cycle through
nail polish remover,
sketch books, hopscotch,
and the swing we installed
on the backyard tree
after the mayor closed
all the playgrounds.

The two-year-old is bubbling
over with excitement.
These weeks quarantined
with him have been everything
Montesorri was not:
Black, mama all day, and free.

This resuscitating joy
and the pink purple sunset
breathe life back into the Bill Withers
songs I've been humming all day
—since, I heard he left.

BAPTISM BY DIRT
for Shauna

All believers know about the power of water
though not enough about the power of dirt.
My mama used to walk barefooted
in our vegetable garden,
get down on her hands and knees
and almost pray in the dirt.
My wife and I and our two-year-old
built and planted three raised-bed gardens.
Watching her dip her fingers into the dirt
to coddle what will feed us
reminds me of mama and then.

What is it that women know
about nurturing a seed into a piece of fruit,
about believing in the power of dirt
and suns and water?

I return from our labor with sore knees
and back, fingernails and hands caked with dirt.
She floats back into the house cleaner,
somehow less burdened,
as if she spent the weekend
burying all her heavy things,
as if she whispered to something sacred
and it whispered   something back.

TO THE TEN-YEAR-OLD KID ON A VENTILATOR

The coronavirus sucks, don't it?
I bet you miss your friends and even school,
right now.

This wasn't supposed to be the test you dreaded,
one you never had a chance to prepare for.

You're supposed to be counting down
the remaining days 'til summer, rushing to be first
in line not the first child in critical condition.

All I remember about fifth grade
was my first pair of thick glasses
and memorizing the Gettysburg Address.

That hardly compares to a global pandemic,
and shelter-in-place, but being stuck inside
probably sounds better than being stuck by needles.

I'm sure you'd trade those doctors and nurses
for a knucklehead brother or bothersome sister
right now.

When I was ten, I dreamed about what I wanted
to be when I grew up.
You are in ICU dreaming about having a chance to.

I can't help but feel like we failed you somehow.

BEFORE HASHTAGS

My parents' generation
accessed and summed
the world too.
They got their good news
from the King James,
knew what was happening
from the grapevine,
trusted folk wisdom
more than headlines,
and could discern the truth
from a white
lie before it laced up its shoe.

Today's long, heavy rains
and collective mourning
over the latest lynchings,
over the genocidal undertones
of coronavirus death counts
would likely earn
her forever optimistic,
"It always rains when good people die"
and his more cynical, "it's always raining,
somewhere."
And you would barely hear the clap
or the clap back.

OLD-SCHOOL MATH

Life in most assisted-living
facilities and nursing homes
is just like wintering in Florida
—minus the big house
near the beach, enough money
for a private-duty nurse,
and a kind Jamaican woman
to attend to all your needs.

Though not quite prisoners,
many residents are confined
to hospital beds, barely
ambulatory, or locked forever
out of their own minds
and receive few or no visitors.

Mama checked her own mother
out of the facility where the
siblings had put her. She set up
a hospital bed in our living
room, made us use the back door
to come and go   until granny went.

If she were alive today, Mama would have
a grandmother in every room
and be Clorox-wiping everything
—coronavirus be damned.

She knew poor, broken, and old
did not mean indignity.
And it certainly didn't equal death.

ON MOTHER'S DAY

I'm going to pretend
that mine ain't dead,
that she's just quarantined.

Because she was a nurse
I know she'd be very serious
about social distancing,
hand washing, and the wearing
of masks.

So me and my siblings would
probably plant ourselves
six feet apart
in her backyard,
so that when she got up to
open her blinds and stepped out
onto her balcony
into the sunshine,
we'd all be sitting there
in our lawn chairs, smiling.

Somebody would lead us
in a song, which we'd sing
badly but with all our hearts.

She would blow us kisses
and rain down I love yous.

We'd linger until she made us go
or some other mother's day
pulled us away.

Folks are going to be salty
and complain all day about not
getting to hug their mamas.

Believe me when I tell you,
I really understand.

SEVERE WEATHER WARNING

COVID-19, a silent multi-eyed system, formed in early 2020,
    made landfall, and stalled out over NYC, Chicago, Detroit,
        and New Orleans causing the closing of schools,
            churches, the cancellation of all sporting
                and entertainment events, widespread
            damage to the economy and catastrophic
        loss of life, though physical structures,
        shorelines, and trees have sustained
            zero damage.   No evacuations expected,
                but residents have been ordered
                    to shelter-in-place, wear masks,
                    and follow social distancing
                guidelines at all times.
              If the governor of your
          red state urges
          you to return
           before experts
           say it's safe,
            please know
             it is a trick
                  to erase
            your vote
            by erasing
             you first.

B.C.

Seems like a long time
ago, before the longest
spring break ever,
when you could be
YouTube famous
for something hilarious
or amazing or bizarre.

Today, their biggest wish
is to replicate the newest
TikTok challenge
and to get at least
a little bit of summer.

Before corona,
young people rushed to post
and wanted just a moment
in their lives
—to go viral.

PECULIAR

Enslavement was not a virus,
but the arrogance,
the false sense
of superiority,
and the undervaluing
of everything kissed
by the sun   is.

HAIRLINE FRACTURE
for Taajwar D'van Howard

Now that shelter-at-home
has passed the three-week mark,
I look in the mirror and smile
when I see my grandfather's hairline.
I also see my grown-man son staring back
and very little of me, since I've been mostly bald
for over thirty years—longer than he's been alive.

But not a primping and preening son
who would ever worry about anything as superficial
as hair, but a Vulcan-like logic son, who, in response
to uninvited compliments on his new-look beard
in the much-coveted Tokyo pictures the twins found
on social media, quickly said, in his defense,

"I joined an on-line group called Black in Japan
and asked, but there are no products in the stores
and no black barbers anywhere near me."

It made me laugh then, and running my fingers across
my dome reminds me even now, that I may
or may not partake in some groom for Zoom
today, before throwing on a hat, to distinguish myself
from him and my father's father, however slightly.

I have not seen the inevitable plethora of corona
t-shirts yet, but I'll be looking for one that says,
This hairy beast is not the pandemic me
—I'm just missing my son.

MENDACITY

mendacity [men-das-I-tee]
noun, plural men·dac·i·ties

1. *the quality of being mendacious; untruthfulness; tendency to lie.*
2. *an instance of lying; falsehood.*

DERIVED FORM
mendacious [men-dey-shuhs]
adjective

A *mendacious* person might say, "You can call it a germ, you can call it a flu, you can call it a virus, you know you can call it many different names. I'm not sure anybody even knows what it is."

1. Outright lying in a fast food drive thru and then Biggie-Sizing it, such as *"Nobody knew there would be a pandemic or epidemic of this proportion"* or *"It's going to disappear. One day it's like a miracle—it will disappear."*

2. Telling a bold face lie, without basis, such as *"Americans will have access 'to vaccines, I think, relatively soon."*

3. To improvise, to just make shit up, to raise lying to an art form such as *"Anybody that needs a test gets a test. We—they're there. They have the tests. And the tests are beautiful."*

4. To lie so blatantly it is assumed that you'll go straight to hell so quickly that in that moment one's pants catch on fire, such as *"I've always known this is a real—this is a pandemic. I felt it was a pandemic long before it was called a pandemic. I've always viewed it as very serious."*

5. To distort the truth and then to compound the lie by attempting to distance oneself from it with flat out denials or by casting aspersions such as *"that's a nasty question"* or *"that's fake news"* or deflections like, *"every country spreads lies about the coronavirus,*

what's the big deal?" and then ultimately to shift the blame to others i.e., the previous administration, the Chinese, the liberal media, Andrew Cuomo, et. al.

In the same house as white lie, but significantly whiter, like European colonizer white or Ku Klux Klan robe white. Also see xenophobic white. Often soft-pedaled as simply: dishonesty, prevarication, untruthfulness, hyperbole.

ANTONYM
veracity as in *44 is greater than 45*.

MRS. BUTTERWORTH, UNCLE BEN & AUNT JEMIMA

… walk into a bar in America.
Butterworth says, I'm being repackaged.
Ben says, I'm being rebranded.
Jemima says, I remember
when they branded my mama   on her back.

The bartender says, I could stand in the middle
of Main Street and kill somebody
and I wouldn't lose any voters.
Butterworth says, then I'll take eight bullets
in my sleep. Ben says choke me to death
with your knee. Jemima says,
lock me in a holding cell and say
I decided to hang myself.

The bartender poured the drinks,
said he felt threatened
and was simply standing his ground
when he thought the thug
was reaching for a gun.

The headlines said Well-Loved American
Foods Resisted Arrest, Failed
to Comply, and Were Delicious While Black.

Butterworth's daughter said here's to progress,
we might finally get an anti-lynching bill.
Ben's son said I'd rather they abolish
qualified immunity. Jemima's kid said you know
they abolished slavery once,
then they hung my mama   on that box.

COMPLICIT, AT MOST

I am no more guilty
than the officers' eyes
choosing to look the other way.

Technically, I'm not even touching
his neck. All I could feel
was the hot cotton insides
of officer Chauvin's slacks
against my skin.

Almost nine minutes is a long time,
to kneel, on a neck, especially
if you are unaccustomed
to praying or begging.

But after pressing all of me down
he put this all on me
as if he was planning to propose,
but got cold feet
and was too embarrassed to get up,
and just walk away from this altar-
cation, marrying us both
to this moment, 'til death do us part.

*TO THE WHITE WOMEN WHO FORMED A LINE
BETWEEN BLACK PROTESTORS AND POLICE*

Thanks, but you owed us that.
Your daughters of the confederacy
put up all those monuments
to white supremacy to intimidate us,
and dared to call it heritage not hate.

Almost every slave ship captain,
Confederate officer, Grand Cyclops,
Tulsa-rioter, lynch-mobber,
redliner, gerrymanderer, biased judge,
killer cop, and impeached president
started out as your baby boy.

Anything good about men
is often a credit to their mothers.

Maybe their empire building,
hunger for wealth and power,
appetite for violence,
and need to keep their boot
on somebody's neck
is some misguided effort to gain
your approval or your affection.

Maybe you lost the battle
for their souls to their fathers
who used your neck to sharpen
their canines and bicuspids.

Maybe it put something bitter in the milk.

If you could smell their colicky breaths
again, would you hug them to death?

THE END OF SPORTING

No balls. No teams.
No uniforms.
Just shirts and skins.
Just beautiful Black bodies
in slow motion, 'cause that's why
you watch. Admit it.

A soundtrack of choreographed
almost breathless heartbeats.
3-D 5G Cameras that zoom in and out.
Accent lights and shadows.
Judges that pontificate about
the sweat, the musculature,
the "sanguinacity" of each flight.

Broadcast it live on Pay-Per-View.
Sell season subscriptions.
But don't call it something blithe
like Comply or Obey.
Be honest. Tell the truth.
Call it: Stop, or I'll …

And by stop, you'll mean don't blink.
Don't be Black or brown.
Don't. Even. Breathe. N…
(But you won't even have to say
the N-word   out loud).

READ A BOOK, THEN ASK WHAT YOU CAN DO

If you get hot under the collar when it is suggested
that you had a head start,
or that you were born with an advantage,

if you really believe everything you've achieved
and everything you own is simply a direct result
of your hard work or God's blessing
and that "the blacks" just need to work harder,

if you think that the fact that you're not rich
is the same as four hundred years of oppression,

if you got a college degree and never had to read
a novel by a Black man or woman,

if you first learned that the founding fathers
owned people when you were an adult,

if you don't acknowledge the relationship
between Africa's abundant natural resources
and colonialism or that American wealth
was built on the backs of the enslaved,

if you believe Thomas Jefferson and Sally Hemings'
children are the product of a love story
and not a dirty secret, not rape,

if you find the Nazi swastika offensive
but not the Confederate flag,

if you reach for your wallet when commercials
zoom in on wet, shivering, malnourished dogs,
but don't shed a tear about children in cages
or care if Puerto Ricans or the Navajo

get their COVID-19 relief,
then you will understand my raised brow
when I hear you insist that all lives matter.

OFFENSIVE CAPTAIN

They had become so arrogant
they didn't even change the playbook.
We knew they would try to convince us
we couldn't trust the video
with our own eyes, minds, or hearts.

When the officer called the play in the huddle,
he didn't care that the cameras were on.

BLACK-27. STOP-RESISTING.
AFRAID-FOR-MY-LIFE.
WE-WILL-CALL-IT-SELF-DEFENSE.
'TIL. HE. CAN'T. BREATHE. On three.
BREAK! (Clap)

When he adjusted his knee and called an audible
he believed his offensive guards,
who were compressing the lungs,
were hidden behind the line of scrimmage
as if we'd never seen a fake up the middle,
strong right, quarter-cop sneak.

The sobbing, grief-stricken, collapsing
Black matron on the Jumbotron in the end zone
feels like paid advertising on a loop.

The Cheerleaders are chanting *All Lives Matter*
and *He, he, Should-Have-Obeyed.*
He-should-have-obeyed! in between
the deafening roar of *Go! Big! Blue!*

The first autopsy suggested hypertension
killed the play and not the 8 minute and 46
seconds while the cop took a knee.

We must change the game. We must change it now.
What have we got to lose?

QUALIFIED IMMUNITY

> "… an absolute shield for law enforcement officers."
>
> —Justice Sonia Sotomayor

Doctor Strange had one,
but it was invisible
so you couldn't really hide behind it
like killer cops do.

Most starships like the Enterprise
have the capability
to deploy a force field,
but it doesn't protect murderers
from guilty verdicts
like Qualified Immunity does.

Their old Get-Out-of-Jail-Free cards
have been replaced with
a No-Chance-of-Ever-Even-Going.

It gives police permission
to shoot first and ignore questions later,
to not only use excessive force,
but to kill with impunity.
It is everything but the victim
in the definition
of state-sanctioned violence.

Will justice for Breonna Taylor be
a wrongful-death lawsuit, watered down
from murder or manslaughter,
against three white policemen
becoming the next legal moment
illustrating that in our justice system
the policy is as corrupt as the police?

TWELVE THINGS AMY BELIEVED SHE KNEW

1. The posted park rules were for everybody else.
2. A black man could not tell her what to do or film her not doing it.
3. Central Park was built for white women and dogs and not black bird watchers.
4. If she threatened to call the police the black man would submit or flee.
5. If she made herself sound afraid, breathless, and very vulnerable on the phone the police would come even faster.
6. The primary purpose of the police was to serve and protect *her*.
7. If she said African American enough times the dispatcher would expedite assistance.
8. When the police arrived they wouldn't ask questions.
9. When the officers saw her skin they'd know who was right.
10. They would pull out their guns, extinguish the threat, and say he resisted arrest.
11. Even if people saw the video, nobody would see how well she understood the game.
12. He would lose his freedom or even his life before she lost her dog or her job.

SLEIGHT OF HAND

> "Donald Trump's imprisoned former campaign chairman, released to home confinement for the rest of his sentence amid concerns that he could contract the coronavirus."
>
> —NBC News

Used to be a simple planting of 8.5 oz
or the "discovery" of 5 plants in Kentucky
turned a trumped-up possession
into trafficking, multiplied by X
if within 1000 yards of a school, church,
or park, though everywhere in the hood
is across the street from a house of worship,
and within ten football fields of a school,
though rarely anywhere near a park.

Black lives don't seem to matter when it comes
to stops and searches, arrests, prosecutions
and pleas, trials, and life without parole.

Even before body cameras, that often forget
to turn themselves on when officers
are already titillated over a falling
or somehow swinging black body,

fat cats and wrong-doers with friends
in high places were being released
to home imprisonment
in mansions and condominiums
while Bubba, Juanita, and Tyrell serve every day
of their 5–10 years for felony possession
of a substance that is legal in 11 states.

ODE TO MEAT PACKERS

> "The US has been hardest hit, with outbreaks [of COVID-19] at more than 180 meat and processed foods plants."
>
> —The Guardian

O you of tired feet, sore hands,
weary second-shift eyes,
and darker, minimum-wage skin,
the Executive Order
signed by the President
to keep your plants open,
to keep meat in grocery stores
and on America's tables, despite
the need for more spacing
on your lines,
personal protection equipment,
more sanitizing stations,
and barriers to separate workers,
at least implies you are now essential.

Forget the ICE raids, families
at the border, and children still in cages.
Ignore the prioritizing of beef
over ventilators, pork over vaccines,
and poultry over tests.

Now that it's considered patriotic
for somebody to die for the economy,
take heart. In case you missed out
on a signed stimulus check,
his autograph on the Order
makes it clear that he takes
responsibility this time, and almost

acknowledges your sacrifice
and your place in the supply chain
to satisfy America's appetite.

EASTER PRAYER, 2020 A.C.

All powerful Black Jesus,
please protect my brothers and sisters
and their families and friends
when they gather together, illegally,
to enjoy Easter Dinner and the Sabbath.

May they pass around the sanitizer
after holding hands in prayer.

May whoever is lifting up your name
be wearing a mask correctly, oh Lord.

May any pork that touches their lips
not mess with their blood pressure.

Hide the salt, sweet Jesus, and please grant
them the vision to bring at least one sugar-free
dessert, some diet sodas, and unsweetened tea.

Strengthen them for their fight against
that devil diabetes and all cancers, Lord.

Thank you for their on-time unemployment
checks, Medicaid, and Obama Care.

Help them choose wisely if the choice is between
the cable and light bill, and their life insurance.

And if it is your will to take all they asses
because they refuse to believe COVID-19 is real,
let this be the best meal they ever ate, Lord.

And take them all on the same day, so that they
may offer comfort to each other in the hospital

and allow the rest of us to endure only one drive-through service.

Amen.

FAKE NEWS?

Conservative Court
Justices Vote Remotely
To Deny Wisconsinites
Right To Vote Remotely

Evangelicals Attending
White House Easter Egg
Hunt Witness Resurrection
of White Chocolate Jesus

According to Fox News, one
of these headlines is not true.

MAMASORRI SCHOOL
for Shauna

Thanks to the weekly schedule
posted on the refrigerator,
created by the woman who descends
the stairwell to provide technical support
and change diapers
between Zoom meetings,
still wearing her work voice and title,
our self-directed upper school
and lower school students,
surrounded by African art and natural light,
gather each morning in the dining hall
classroom cafeteria space
after she has baked cinnamon rolls,
made waffles or fruit smoothies,
while the two-year-old rotates
between station one,
where he is currently conducting experiments
in Thomas the Tank Engine coupling
and magnetic polarity,
and station two, where his imagination
has animated DUPLO-sized LEGOs
into fire engines, excavators, tow trucks
and yet another train,
before he builds a tower
from colorful wooden letters of the alphabet
just to knock it down,
or pours out the entire see-through bag
of small wooden instruments
to express himself through music.

The front porch and sidewalk
is an art station on warm days.
On cool days, art happens
in the converted exercise room
which used to be my writing studio
back in 2020 B.C.—Before Corona.

Most mornings I rise early,
wonder about one thing or another,
wander down to the kitchen
for some high-fiber cereal and juice,
social distance myself
in any quiet space I can find
and try to chase these poems,
before the bell rings and I assume my post
as hall monitor, security guard, and PE teacher,
already knowing I'll have to stay
after school.

I'M BEING SARCASTIC

Our two-year-old grabbed the mic,
pronounced his uneaten slice
of watermelon a "boat" and sailed it
off his plate onto the dark blue sea
table mat, becoming the after dinner
entertainment instead of the evening
press conference.

And as soon as we were all convinced
he was right, he picked it up, smiled slyly,
took two quick bites and pronounced it
a "race car."

I thought, "my God, he could be president,"
as I imagined him in a big red tie
instead of his signature bib, the second ever
toddler to take a dump in the Oval Office.

We all thought telling little white lies
and dressing up like a clown was cute until
the German kid opened up her real science kit.

Our problem child makes unflyable paper planes
out of the constitution, uses fat crayons to color
his talking points, pretends to know more
than all the experts, and waits for the adults
in the room to clean up his latest mess.

COMBUSTIBLES
after Amiri Baraka

Who already sick and tired
of the planned new normal?
Who want change?
Who demand justice now?
Who know they lives matter?
Who die the most
at the hands of cops?

Who speak riot
sing protest and shout uprising?
Who they say "loot"
and be made to look less righteous?
Who set police cars ablaze?
Who grieve with bricks,
water bottles, and fire?
Who eat pepper spray,
flash bangs, and tear gas
for dinner?
Who say defund the police
and fuck their curfew?
Who burn the Target
and the precinct down?
Who ready   to be
the next hashtag?

DEEJAY BATTLE

> "When the looting starts, the shooting starts."
>
> —President DJ Trump

The oppressors' private property
is always more important
to the privileged. Their power
is what police protect,

backed by a national guard
fronting a commander-in-cheat
known to incite and encourage
violence against POC by the FOP
and other 'good people' vs 'thugs.'

If you don't understand
'this behavior'
or 'these people',
you don't understand
emotional or psychological trauma.
You don't understand
generational grief.

And you really don't understand
injustice or American history.

Know justice. Know peace.
No justice. No peace.
No just ICE raids.
No guilty cops, just us,
dead, dying, and chalk marked
over and over again,
like some wack DJ, rewinding
the bridge or dead refrain,
scratching   at our eyes

with already viral,
breathless, black-body porn
professionally made
by the hands, feet and now knees
of thug police, again.

Instead of turning the tables
we drag out turntables
and spin and spin and spin
searching old wax, seeking to sample
something human,
anything truly good to mix
with this Black,
in our Lives,
until we Matter.

Y'ALL SAY I DO, WE SAY BLACK LIVES MATTER
for Kerry-Anne and Michael

What a powerful way to say 'til death
do us part. To stand in defiance of murder
after murder after murder and still choose life,
together. To seal your vows and then march

for all our promises, into Philly streets,
swollen with protestors, where they replaced rice
with tear gas and pepper spray; It still felt
more like a large reception for freedom than a riot.

Resplendent in wedding gown and tuxedo,
fists raised high to demonstrate that
Black Love is the Liberation married
to the joy that fills your faces,

thinking only of the honeymoon where all couples
know justice because Black couples know peace.

THE FAITHFUL

> "He didn't say that. And if he did, he didn't mean that.
> And if he did, it's not a big deal. And if it is, others have
> said worse."
>
> —Anonymous Trump loyalist

I can't say I understand, but I can say I've seen it.
Almost blind loyalty to a man you believe in,
one who praised your belief, who made you feel seen.
A man who stared at your imperfections and convinced
you they were beauty marks, making it easier for you
to look away, to be forgiving, when you finally saw his.

My mother believed, once, for a long time. She refused
to see any fault, to hear any criticism, to doubt a man,
until he finally crossed the line. Her God did not condone
the exploitation of children, the violation of young boys.

She was devout, so she prayed and she prayed.
She refused to judge. And she prayed on it some more.
Then she remembered she had little boys at home too.

So, I don't question such belief. And I try not to judge, but
I can't help but worry about where they've drawn the line.

A NEW WORD ORDER

Social distancing and masks before
"this is their new hoax."
Empathy before victim blaming.
Assist before assault.
Bridges before walls.
Equity and inclusion
before institutional racism.
Make a difference
before make a profit.
"I knew how bad it was"
before "it's hard not to be happy
with the job we're doing."
And the former administration
before this one.

COLONIZER-13

This is not the first
endemic American virus.

Manifest Destiny
wiped out and displaced
whole nations
of indigenous peoples
—and stole their land.

DIRTY DOZEN
for David McAtee

You could plant a whole field
of tobacco.
You could visit every distillery tour
in the state in that half-day.
You could watch the morning workout
and catch a full day of racing
at Churchill Downs or Keeneland.
UofL and UK could play
four Governor's Cups.
You could drive the full length
of the bluegrass and back and stop and eat
at two different Cracker Barrels.
You could feed a family of five for one week
on a dozen hours of minimum-wage pay.

Or send national guard troops
using lethal rounds to enforce a curfew
by shooting and killing a black man
in the door of his own restaurant,
several miles from the downtown protests,
and leave his body in the street
—for twelve hours.

MASKED MAN, BLACK
after Paul Laurence Dunbar

Black male me walks into a store
in broad daylight black phone in hand
wearing a black mask.

You already know how this ends.
Somebody felt threatened.
Somebody got shot.
Black woman wailing makes news.

But it isn't new.
All the chalk outlines are white.
All the states are red.
The coronavirus doesn't discriminate.
Racists still do.

Peel off mask no grins no lies.

TO THE MAN WHO WORE A KLAN HOOD TO THE GROCERY STORE …

in response to the state mandated
order to wear masks in public.
Big props for your cosplay,
though your effort to dress up
as a favorite character in the tone-setting
Birth of a Nation, Gone With the Wind,
Blazing Saddles, O Brother, Where Art Thou?,
Mississippi Burning, A Time to Kill,
Django Unchained, Bad Boys II,
and *Watchmen* might be a stretch
without the robe,
though the authentic-looking mullet
and camouflage shirt was a notable
expression of the depth of your fandom.

If we ever see you and your friends
out together in full costume and character,
it's great to know   you're just playing.

TO THE MAN SPEWING SPIT AND VITRIOL IN THE TROOPER'S FACE AT THE CAPITOL

Expressing so much passion towards a woman
who is not even there, a kiss away from a man
who pretends that you're not there either,
has to be a whole chapter in the *S&M Guide
to the Universe: a Sex Manual for Broken Men.*

Maybe the ever-present Confederate flags
are constant reminders of a time when a noose,
and the rope that birthed it, was not intended
for the woman you pay to bind you at night,

but for bad hombres and n-words you fear
she dreams about. Maybe you handcuff her
because the police academy rejected you too,
and when you role-play, she is Emmett Till
or Trayvon or another 14-year-old boy.

But that would make you a pedophile
and you ain't sick, just angry at a woman
who you believe locked you up too tight,
stripped you of your liberties,
made you feel like three-fifths of a man,

except for the massive gun you are carrying,
—which is not about overcompensation *per se*,
but about expressing the freedoms you claim
you no longer have, because a woman in the state
House gave you no choice, took something precious
and sacred from you without your consent
or before you could agree on a safe word.

HYPOCRITES AND OATHS
for Healthcare Workers

My mother was a nurse. If you know one,
you know how hard they work. You know
how emotionally taxing it can be to do
what they do for such long hours every day.

To offer comfort, compassion and care
to whoever shows up and their families,
to use personal phones during this pandemic
so loved ones can say goodbye is Jesus work.
It's not work I could ever do.

I could always look at her face and know
when she witnessed someone in her care
not make it. You could hear it in her voice.
You could see it in her eyes. She carried
the weight of it around in her bones.

There are people who have been made to believe
the coronavirus is a hoax. Before they "liberate"
their state houses, they should sit with a nurse
at the end of a shift. They should carry
body bags to the waiting trucks. They should help
dig the mass graves in New York City.

They have the right to believe shelter-in-place
orders are tied to gun rights and abortion issues.
They have a right to their Confederate flags
and racist views.

But when they find themselves on death's door
or wanting a painless transition for loved ones,
will they accept the care of a competent Black nurse
or wait for a tweet from their real estate agent?

WANT ADS

HELP WANTED. Nonsmoking,
hygienically-conscious,
COVID-negative surrogate to
serve as public persona
for hyper-allergic professional.
Must be willing to shake hands.
Some sanitizing experience preferred.
Anti-vaxers need not apply.

Athletic, middle-aged man
SEEKING same for occasional
foursome. Must be at least six
months COVID-19 free and have
a single digit handicap.

FOR SALE. Home ventilator kit.
Slightly used. Comes with
military grade hand sanitizer.
Eleven months still remaining
on warranty.

SEASON TICKET HOLDERS

Before the pandemic, feeding the birds
was little more than a chore. I appreciated
their beauty from our window, and I noticed
how quickly the birdseed disappeared.

Now, filling the feeder is part of a morning ritual
with our two-year-old, and we've got floor seats
to the daily races between the pair of cardinals,
bluejays, doves, and a red-headed woodpecker.

At the opposite end of the court are the pick-up games
between the athletic sparrows and the neighborhood's
feral felines. It feels a little strange because
for the first time in a long time, I'm not rooting for the cats.

I do miss my comfortable chair, ESPN, Game Day,
and a cold beer, but what I'm modeling for my son
has made me a less unruly fan and a much better father.

TOO SOON?

So, a smallpox blanket,
a Tuskegee experiment,
and a Republican governor
all walk into a bar in Atlanta...

It seems that everything,
even the dark and the difficult,
was funnier before COVID-19
—if left to real comedians.

Dave Chappelle's blind,
black klansman skit
interrogated the complexities
of race and the irrationality
of American racism.

Richard Pryor's personal struggle
with addiction offered up humor
born out of darkness and pain.

They were rarely silly and goofy
for saccharin's sake.

Never mean-spirited, targeting
someone less fortunate just for laughs.

Making comedy self-deprecating
without becoming minstrelsy
is an art form, is a gift.

We won't know if we can really survive
the coronavirus until somebody
makes a joke, and it only hurts   a little.

EXODUS?

> "We the generation ... trod through great tribulation"
> —Bob Marley

This could be our Babylon, our Egypt. We're living
in a remake of a classic, with a reality TV star in the role
of Pharaoh, and plagues of incompetence, ignorance,
divisiveness, arrogance and greed traumatizing
the people and the land.

This neo-Ramses, wearing too much stage makeup,
prone to abandon the script and create his own lines
and truths, has made a shambles of the Constitution
and the Commandments.

No more separation of church and state, no more checks
and balances. His god is money. He and his cronies stole
an election. He idolizes Putin, golfs on Sundays, sleeps
with porn stars, covets his own daughter, and bears false
witness in full-page ads in the New York Times. He lies
about a pandemic that is killing thousands every day.

He is not a stable genius, but probably smart enough
to know that Yul Brynner was Russian too.

If Hollywood could pretend that Egypt wasn't in Africa,
if Charlton Heston could play the Hebrew Moses,
then liars can "lead" and Slovenian models can play Nefertiti.

But if the Surgeon General is the court jester, and science
and truth have been exiled, where do we, who have known
hardship and strife, find our Moses?

STORMY FORECAST

Last night, at the height of the drama,
it was me perched by the open window,
listening for sirens, worried the ominous sound
and wind was more than the thunderstorm
that seemed to park itself in our backyard.

After checking all the doors and windows again,
I wondered about the pair of cardinals
and the humble sparrows that breakfast
at our kitchen window. I thought about the smallest
of birds roosting upstairs in the still half-naked trees.

When the sky burst open again with crackling
search lights, with momentary sun followed
by a deep-throated rumble that shook everything
in the house, did they squeeze their perches tighter,
tuck their heads under their wings and huddle
beneath the covers like we did?

Did they waste a moment contemplating fear
and humility or simply dream of the fat worms
the rain would coax out, grateful for the synchronicity
and power of spring storms and their need
for fresh nesting supplies?

When they sing back daylight, unlock
their throats and call us up a new sun,
will they simply have slept through it all

or will they regret their anxiety-ridden
terse exchanges traded in the night,
the too-real dreams made darker
by the evening news and worry, even a little,
about who in their tree will be taking their last flight?

A JOYFUL NOISE

Mama, a charismatic minister for twenty-two years,
might scoff, at first, if she called and asked
where I was and I replied, "church."

But this, and every Sunday morning since
the pandemic response in Kentucky outlawed
mass gatherings, Christ Temple New Assembly
church directly across the street from our house
moved its services outdoors into their parking lot.

My reading chair in the corner of the bedroom
may as well be a wooden pew in the second row
of the sanctuary, especially when, instead of hands
clapping to make a joyful noise, those assembled
enthusiastically press car horns in praise.

Our double-paned glass windows, hollow doors,
and concrete siding are anemic Davids
to the 500 Watts, 127 decibel Goliath sound system
drowning out any competition from the devices
in our domain, making non-attendance not an option
along with the impossibility of our toddler's nap.

"Wherever two or more are gathered in my name,"
made no provision for amplification.

Whatever expansion plans church elders had
for their temple have likely been more than realized
now that their music, prayers, scripture readings,
sermons, and power can be experienced
for blocks in every direction.

THE APPRENTICESHIP WRECK

I cannot watch the daily body count,
the eighteen-wheeler street-side morgues,
the mass burials of unclaimed bodies
or the blame game and daily train wreck
from the White House.

I am too stricken with grief about the under
preparedness, the tardy response,
and colossal missteps that continue
and only serve to compound the sorrow.

It already feels like a month-long funeral
with a snake oil salesman or dime store preacher
interrupting the eulogy to pat himself on the back,
while trying to convince grieving families
that this was the best funeral ever.

And the only thing Americans can agree on
is that he didn't really know the deceased
and how unpresidential it feels to insist
on autographing obituaries.

CITIUS, ALTIUS, FORTIUS, A.C.

Is this the future?
Football stadiums with no fans.
Basketball arenas and empty seats.
Where is our imagination?
Where is our vision?

Install a camera in every seat.
Offer that point of view to ticket holders,
family members, and the press.

No more nosebleed sections
where the patrons watch
the big screen instead of the field.
No more privileged sideline and half-court
seats exclusively for money and power.
Instead of ticket scalping,
encourage pay what you can.
Transform seats into real time images
of every player's loved ones and friends.
Make the NCAA pay for it.

No more athletic prowess sacrificed
for the pleasure of strangers.
Let the competition not be reduced
to gladiators risking death
for their own freedom, for mere spectacle
at the pleasure of owners, athletic directors, and VIPs.

Let it be something more.
Something truly laudable and untaintable.
Something that brings back the spirit of the game,
for the love of the game. Something
that highlights the honor in victory and defeat.

We can run faster. We can reach higher.
We can be stronger. Let us.

SCIENTIFIC DOUBT

I believe in science   enough
to wash my hands and wear a mask,
and too much to think
"that one day soon it will all
just magically disappear"
—without a vaccine.

I'm afraid of what scientists
refer to as a "second wave,"
another outbreak of coronavirus,
that would hit us in the fall
and infect fifty percent
of the population,
followed by a third round next spring
that would get everybody else.

I'm afraid that in a rush
to get back to "normal,"
to "open up the economy"
ahead of the presidential election,
that people will hurry back out there,
forget about the social distancing
that helped flatten the curve,
and provoke a longer shelter-in-place order,
another toilet paper shortage,
an early end to summer, more funerals,
and a delayed start of school.

Fall is still too far away to speculate
if we will return to our classrooms,
if there will be fans in the stands,
if big marching bands

will even be allowed to practice,
if the virus will kill the World Series,
if everything delayed will just die.

Will we finally embrace national restoration
of voting rights for "returning citizens,"
mail-in ballots, and homeschool,
or be convinced that natural selection
trumps science and death is just the cost
of doing business   in America?

LIKE MOBY-DICK, BUT BIGGER

If the Donald is indeed
this young century's Ahab
singularly focused
on his great white self,

let people, united,
be the shining sea
rising up to drown him out.

Let COVID be the harpoon
that finally drags his
blubbery superego
to the surface,

and allow his willingness
to let so many die
for corporate profits
and his reelection
wash him overboard
in November.

SIX FEET UNDER, SIX APART

> "It is strongly recommended that, until further notice, funerals be limited to no more than 10 of the decedent's immediate family members."
>
> —The National Funeral Directors Association

I suppose the occasion would call
for a selfie with the deceased
to serve as a memorial.

Each of the ten must function
as an officiant, pallbearer,
eulogist, offerer of song
or prayer, performer of the last
rites, the somber face
that greets and seats.

We would rotate viewing,
being careful to maintain
the mandatory distance
between us before lowering
the body
the same distance under.

Military funeral protocol
would eliminate the flag
and requisition an origami
version of the program
folded into a triangle
by a uniformed soldier
wearing white latex gloves,
while a recording of taps
played on someone's phone.

The invitees would be named
in the will, determined by lottery,
or the roll of a die. Vacant spots
could be regifted or sold on eBay
to mourners still seeking closure
from previous passings.

I leave my ten to my three seeds,
of course, the twins, my widow,
a fraternity brother, a young Black
poet, anybody who can play a sax,
and the artist who designed
the kente funeral masks.

REVISIONIST HISTORY

My father did not go
to his own sister's funeral.
I'm sure he wanted to,
but three time zones
is a long while to be strapped
to a little, hard chair
in the same narrow room
breathing the same air
somebody you don't even know
"done already breathed."

I think he knew I was serious
when I offered to drive him there
and back, but I also know
he was too proud to say yes.
Real, hard-earned independence
in his generation dies hard.

I now know he was just teaching
us how to prepare for a pandemic.
He was modeling how to gather
all that emotional baggage
and do something positive with it.

Zoom hadn't been invented,
so we just planted a tree.
Some thought him odd, a little quirky,
but he was just ahead of his time.

REMEMBER TO BREATHE

I don't like to worry. I don't like to leave things
up to chance. I learned from somewhere
that prior planning prevents poor performance.

Such behavior must have been drilled into me
or possibly encoded for my own survival,
because this new not knowing what's next
feels like the world is piling rocks on my chest.

Every week of the shut-down has felt like
a rope around me that gets tighter every time
I watch the news, or go online, or hear from family.

Never had issues being still when it was just an option.
I'm not ready to march on the capitol. COVID-19 rules
don't register as oppressive to me, but as conspiracy
theories go, this could be an international social
experiment, population control, or just pure genocide.

I believe we all need a chance to decompress,
so I call for a new national holiday with no bad news.
Boycott every media outlet. Unplug the phone.
Don't answer the door. Don't even turn on the TV.

I remember Psychology 101. If we don't take
this holiday, it's just a matter of time before we turn
on each other   like rats.

O DEATH

After a tear-stained winter
with three family funerals,
you stretched your neck
and took a basketball icon
and his daughter,
a black man jogging, another and another,
and then the gifted lyricist
who brought us Grandma's Hands.

You took a young queen in her sleep
before the public lynching of a gentle giant.
You have been more stubborn this year
than the weeds we twist out
of the ground and from between bricks,
returning for more and more
before we can even say their names.

While our cucumbers shriveled on the vine,
you took JackieRobinson/ ThurgoodMarshall
and JamesBrown/KingT'Challa
all over again, all at the same time
when you came for their medium
with a kind of blight he battled privately.

It's not even flu season.
Yet, like our sunflower raised from seed,
threatening to reach her namesake,
your hunger seems to know no bounds.

Studying the former tiny plants turned bushes,
wild green things growing and stretching out
in every conceivable direction,
I watch every bright, yellow bloom slow

into an almost bursting fruit
full of summer showers and sunlight.
Everyone we pluck from the vine
is replaced with another and another and another.

Watching the large, now-yellow leaves fall away
from the heads of cabbages knitting themselves
into almost spinning globes,
into two rows of blue-green planets,
I ask the air around me: what is the lesson here?
What nugget of wisdom am I missing?

Granted, all of this started as a box of dirt.
We made (w)holes and filled them with hope.
They reached for stars and followed the sun every day.
Rested at night. Most of them fed us.
A few shone bright like comets before crashing
into the dirt to become one with the earth again.

O Death, life can't be this painful, beautiful, and simple.
Can it?

LAISSEZ LES BON TEMPS ROULER

They traced the Chicago spike backwards
to a funeral and a birthday party.

In New Orleans it was Mardi Gras,
where COVID-19's invisible krewe
let the good times roll from host to host,

exploiting our love of community, our need
to fall into a circle and breathe each other's air,
keeping the flambeau alive.

Social distancing feels so alien to those
who love family reunions, to those who live
to barbeque, to celebrate each other's
milestones, no matter how small.

How can our greatest strength
also be a weakness?

It's ironic that it all started with loving hellos.
And what's killing us now is not getting to say
goodbye.

2020 VISION

for young white protestors

Even though your grandparents fear
that if we ever get in power
we would do to them
exactly what's been done to us
these last 400 years,
you got close enough to know
we are more human than that.

You read the history
and saw through the lies of heritage
not hate, as their heroes
supported a regime you've watched
deny science and climate change,
destroy the environment,
put children in cages,
profit from the oppression of others,
legislate women's bodies,
buy and steal elections,
wrap their failures in a flag,
hide their sins behind a cross,
sacrifice their moral authority and ethics
at the altar of a man who promised
to make them feel great again.

Or maybe you discovered on your own
that greatness is something earned,
in these streets, not a birthright,
not an honorific you give yourself.

CORONA LOVE
for Shauna

Our stay-at-home order has come with a silver lining.
Suddenly, we can take our time with things that matter,
with everything we may have taken for granted.

Saturday, for example, my wife and I made love,
all day. Now, I don't mean we locked ourselves in
our bedroom for hours and hours, stayed naked
and ... you know.

I mean, all the kids slept in, so we didn't rush either.
We took our time. We kissed. I mean really kissed.
No pecks. No smooches. We kissed. Deep. And long.
And we meant it.

I have to admit that the way the machine ran around here,
pre-corona, we were lucky to get a peck in before getting
four of us off in four different directions to four different
places all before 8A.M.

A measly peck, on those mornings, had to last all day. So,
we didn't just kiss. We lingered in each other's arms,
a place we found ourselves still clinging to after digesting
the previous day's body count and news.
Trying to verbalize our worst fears as the headlines
got closer and closer to our front door, we savor everything
now. We know that if one of us gets sick, there will be nothing
but difficult choices to follow.

If any of our kids were stricken and we were told we couldn't
be at their bedside, what then?

We hugged and flirted through breakfast. We held hands. Sent private messages. Planned a naked nap to coincide with our two-year-old's sleep time.

The few we know who are dying will soon become many.

We know there will be more funerals we can't attend. The impending loss is so heavy, it's hard to keep convincing the teenagers that the homework which used to feel like life and death is just that serious right now.

So we smile and wink and touch and hug and kiss and squeeze and cry and laugh every chance we get. We don't know what's coming and who's going, or if we will be among them. So take our advice:

If you wake up already where you want to be, and don't have to rush anywhere, recognize it as a gift. Take your time. Linger. Wallow. Forget finishing. Don't stop. Leave a tender bookmark. And come back as soon as you can.

ACKNOWLEDGMENTS

I would like to thank the journals who published the earliest versions of the following poems. "Combustibles," "Fake News," "Like Moby-Dick, But Bigger," 'Silver Lining," "Sleight of Hand," and "The Walking Dead" appeared in *Still: The Journal*. "Baptism by Dirt," "Commencement 2020," "DeeJay Battle," "Hairline Fracture," "On Mother's Day," "Y'all Say I Do, and We Say Black Lives Matter" appeared in *The Appalachian Review*. "Mrs. Butterworth, Uncle Ben & Aunt Jemima" and "Complicit, At Most" were published in *Aunt Chloe: A Journal of Artful Candor*, and "Masked Man, Black," "Ode to Meat Packers," "Corona Love," and "Hypocrites and Oaths," appeared in *Sheltering Blue: the Kentucky Pandemic Anthology*.

ABOUT THE AUTHOR

A native of Danville, Kentucky, Frank X Walker is the first African American writer to be named Kentucky Poet Laureate. Walker has published ten collections of poetry, including *Last Will, Last Testament*, winner of the 2020 Judy Gaines Young Book Award, *Turn Me Loose: The Unghosting of Medgar Evers*, which was awarded the 2014 NAACP Image Award for Poetry and the Black Caucus American Library Association Honor Award for Poetry. He is also the author of *Buffalo Dance: The Journey of York*, winner of the 2004 Lillian Smith Book Award, and *Isaac Murphy: I Dedicate This Ride*, which he adapted for stage, earning him the Paul Green Foundation Playwrights Fellowship Award. His poetry was also dramatized for the Contemporary American Theater Festival and staged by Message Theater.

Voted one of the most creative professors in the south, Walker coined the term "Affrilachia" and co-founded the Affrilachian Poets, subsequently publishing the much-celebrated eponymous collection. His honors also include a 2004 Lannan Literary Fellowship for Poetry, the 2008 and 2009 Denny C. Plattner Award for Outstanding Poetry in Appalachian Heritage, the 2013 West Virginia Humanities Council's Appalachian Heritage Award, the 2020 Donald Justice Poetry Award, as well as fellowships and residences with Cave Canem, the National Endowment for the Humanities, and the Kentucky Arts Council. The recipient of honorary doctorates from University of Kentucky, Transylvania University, Spalding University and Centre College, Walker is the founding editor of *pluck! The Journal of Affrilachian Arts & Culture*, Professor of English and African American and Africana Studies, and Director of the Creative Writing program at the University of Kentucky in Lexington.

OTHER BOOKS BY FRANK X WALKER

Eclipsing a Nappy New Millennium, Editor (1997)

Affrilachia (2000)

Buffalo Dance: The Journey of York (2004)

Black Box (2006)

America! What's My Name?, Editor (2007)

When Winter Come: The Ascension of York (2008)

Isaac Murphy: I Dedicate This Ride (2010)

Turn Me Loose: The Unghosting of Medgar Evers (2013)

About Flight (2015)

Affrilachian Sonnets (2016)

Ink Stains & Watermarks: New and Uncollected Poems (2017)

Last Will, Last Testament (2019)